Getting Around

Betsey Chessen • **Daniel Moreton**

Scholastic Inc.

New York • **Toronto** • **London** • **Auckland** • **Sydney**

Acknowledgments

Literacy Specialist: Linda Cornwell

Social Studies Consultant: Barbara Schubert, Ph.D.

Design: Silver Editions

Photo Research: Silver Editions

Endnotes: Jacqueline Smith

Endnote Illustrations: Anthony Carnabucia

Photographs: Cover: Poulides/Thatcher/Tony Stone Images; p. 1: Mark Newman/International Stock Photography; p. 2: (l) Will & Deni McIntyre/Tony Stone Images; (r) Scott Barrow/International Stock Photography; p. 3: (l) Hollenbeck Photography/International Stock Photography; (r) Richmond/The Image Works; p. 4: Jean Higgins/Envision; pp. 5, 9: Jon Spaull/Panos Pictures; p. 6: Hollenbeck Photography/International Stock Photography; p. 7: Poulides/Thatcher/Tony Stone Images; p. 8: Gary Bigham/International Stock Photography; p. 10: Jean Higgins/Envision; pp. 11, 12: Ron Giling/Panos Pictures.

Library of Congress Cataloging-in-Publication Data
Chessen, Betsey, 1970-
Getting around/Betsey Chessen, Daniel Moreton.
p.cm. -- (Social studies emergent readers)
Summary: Simple text and photographs present various ways to get around, including bikes, planes, and donkeys.
ISBN 0-439-04552-5 (pbk.: alk. paper)
1. Transportation--Juvenile literature.
[1. Transportation.] I. Moreton, Daniel. II. Title. III. Series.
TA1149.C454 1998
629--dc21   98-53117
                                                                              CIP AC

4   5   6   7   8   9   10   08   03   02   01   00   99

Transportation

It's how you get around.

By foot.

By bike.

By boat.

By plane.

By skis.

By donkey.

By train.

By bus.

Traffic jam!

Getting Around

Transportation is how people get from place to place. Transportation can take place on land, in the water, or in the air. The types of transportation people use depend on where they live, what means are available, and how far they need to go.

By foot People began walking on two feet at least 3.5 million years ago. Today most people use faster means of transportation. The Amish, a religious people in the U.S. and Canada, still get from place to place on foot. They practice traditional farming methods, wear simple clothes, use no electricity, and do not drive cars (only horse-drawn buggies are allowed).

By bike Bicycles are popular for many reasons. Bikes are less expensive than other kinds of vehicles, and they don't pollute the air. And you don't get stuck in traffic when you ride a bike. In the Western African nation of Sierra Leone, many people use bicycles because gasoline is expensive and the roads are too bad for cars. In countries like China, people use bicycles every day to get to work or do their shopping. China has more bikes than any other country in the world; they produce over 40 million bikes a year.

By boat Boats and ships are very important means of transportation. Hong Kong, a small city under Chinese control, has a busy port. Ships carry goods in and out; ferries carry people from their homes on the tiny surrounding 235 islands to their jobs on the main island; and houseboats provide homes for thousands of people.

By plane People tried to fly for many years before Orville and Wilbur Wright made the first successful flight in North Carolina almost 100 years ago. The first passenger planes that were introduced after World War I took 20 hours to cross the U.S. (today it takes about 6 hours). The largest

passenger plane in the world today is the Boeing 747-400, which can carry 570 passengers. The fastest plane today is the Concorde, which can go from London to New York in three hours!

By skis Skis allow people to move along the snow without sinking in. People first used them in Scandinavia about 3,000 years ago. Until 150 years ago, skiing was not a sport but an important means of transportation in snowy places. Even today, skis are necessary for getting around in isolated places. In some areas of the Alps and Scandinavia, children get to school on skis and postmen use them to deliver the mail.

By donkey Donkeys are a good form of transportation in mountainous areas because they are so sure-footed and can go long distances without needing water or rest. Colombia, South America, has the huge Andes mountain range running right through it, so road and rail systems are difficult and expensive to develop. Donkeys are still the best way to get around parts of that country.

By train Until about 170 years ago, transportation was slow. Horse-drawn carriages traveled at about seven miles per hour. The first steam locomotives, which could pull a "train" of cars at almost 30 m.p.h., changed all that. Railways became faster, safer, and easier to operate. Railroad tracks are everywhere around the world and are still a very important means of transportation.

By bus Buses—another form of public transportation—carry many people from place to place. Until a century ago, buses were pulled by horses, but now they either run on diesel or electric power. In the Philippines, a special kind of bus called a jeepney is the most common form of public transportation. After World War II, American army jeeps were converted into buses. These vehicles are capable of carrying up to 15 passengers.

Traffic jam Transportation today is easier in a lot of ways than it has been in the past. But in some ways it's harder, too. There are more people today, and many more cars, buses, and trucks. Traffic jams are a problem in almost every big city.